The Samosa Thief

Story by Narinder Dhami
Pictures by Tony Blundell

OXFORD
UNIVERSITY PRESS

When Mum made samosas, everyone wanted one. The twins, Sunita and Sanjay, thought Mum's samosas were great.

So did Dad and their older brother Raj.
So did Grandma and Grandpa.

Even the dog Benji loved them! The samosas
never lasted very long!

One Saturday, Mum was in the kitchen making samosas. Sunita and Sanjay were in the garden playing with Benji.

The window was open, and the twins could smell the samosas cooking. Benji could smell them too. His nose was twitching!

Sunita and Sanjay were very hungry. They ran into the kitchen and asked Mum if they could have a samosa.

"Not yet," Mum replied. "You'll have to wait until they cool down a bit."

"But we're really hungry!" said Sanjay.
"My tummy's turning inside-out!" said Sunita.

Mum laughed. "Have an apple," she said.
She put the eight samosas on a plate, and left
them to cool on the shelf.

9

"Let's go and play football with Benji,"
Sanjay said. The twins went back into the
garden, but Benji had gone inside to sleep.

Sanjay and Sunita were kicking the ball around when they heard a shout.

"My samosas!" Mum cried. "They've gone!"

Everyone rushed into the kitchen.
"It can't be Benji," said Mum. "He wouldn't be able to reach the shelf. So who ate them?"

"It wasn't us," said Sanjay and Sunita.
Dad, Raj, Grandma and Grandpa said they
hadn't eaten the samosas either.

"Maybe we can find out who the samosa thief is," Sunita said to Sanjay.

The twins went all over the house, looking for clues.

Dad was in the garage.

Raj was in his bedroom.

Grandma and Grandpa were watching TV. But the twins couldn't find out who'd eaten the samosas.

"I've got an idea!" said Sanjay. "Let's ask Dad to use his new video camera."

The twins asked Mum to make some more samosas. She made six, and put them on a plate to cool.

Sanjay put the video camera on the shelf
near the samosas. Then Dad showed Sunita
how to turn the camera on.

"The camera will record what happens," Sanjay grinned. "Now we'll find out who the samosa thief is!"

The twins went out into the garden. Mum went to the shop, Dad was in the garage and Raj was in his bedroom. Grandma and Grandpa were still watching TV.

After a while, the twins went back to the kitchen.

"Look!" Sanjay shouted, "All the samosas have gone!"

Sunita took the video camera off the shelf.

"Now we can find out who the thief is!" she said.

The twins told everyone to come and watch the video. Even Benji came!

Everyone watched the TV. They saw Benji trot into the kitchen.

Benji could smell the samosas high above his head.

He pushed one of the chairs over to the shelf and jumped onto it.

Now he could reach the samosas, and he ate them all!

Everyone laughed, even Mum.

"Benji, we never guessed it was you!" said Sunita.

"Benji is a very clever dog," said Sanjay.

"And greedy too!" Mum smiled. "No dinner for you tonight, Benji!"